Snowboarding

Larry Dane Brimner

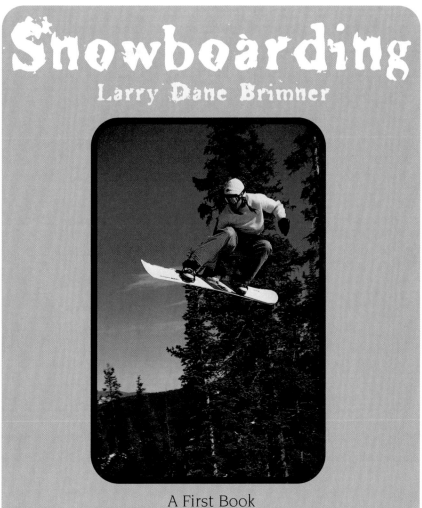

A First Book
Franklin Watts
A Division of Grolier Publishing
New York   London   Hong Kong   Sydney
Danbury, Connecticut

For my young friends in Dolores, Colorado—summer 1996.

Readers are reminded not to snowboard beyond their ability. A book is limited in the amount of technique and advice it can impart, so the author strongly suggests that you enroll in a snowboarding course for the personal attention that it will offer. Neither the author nor the publisher will take any responsibility or liability for injuries resulting from the use of snowboarding equipment.

Photographs ©: Burton Snowboards: 15; L.D. Brimner: 6; Outside Images: 8, 23, 29, 40, 42, 47 (Bob Allen), cover (Doug Berry), 44 (Jamie Bloomquist), 4, 12, 20, 35, 50, 52, 53, 55 (Gary Hubbell), 49 (Patrick Colquhoun), 1, 26, 30, 37, 38, 56 (Bill Thomas).

Library of Congress Cataloging-in-Publication Data

Brimner, Larry Dane.
    Snowboarding / by Larry Dane Brimner.
        p. cm. – (A First book)
    Includes bibliographical references (p.) and index.
    Summary: Traces the history of this recreational activity, describes the required equipment and basic techniques, concludes with a discussion of safety issues and competitive aspects of the sport.
    ISBN 0–531–20313–1
    1. Snowboarding-Juvenile literature. [1. Snowboarding.] I. Title. II. Series
GV857.S57B75 1997
796.9—dc21
                                        97–8962
                                         CIP
                                          AC

Contents Contents Contents Contents

How It Began

What international sport borrows from skateboarding, surfing, and skiing but is defiantly different from each of them? Snowboarding. A snowboard might be described as an oversized skateboard without wheels, a surfboard that surfs frozen waves, or a chubby ski that has lost its companion, for certainly a snowboard resembles all these things. But a snowboard is unique unto itself.

Snowboarding is a relatively new sport. Its history can be traced back to the mid-1960s when an American surfer named Sherman Poppen designed the "Snurfer." He sold his idea to the Brunswick Sporting Goods Company, which sold more than a million Snurfers at about fifteen dollars each.

Snowboarding got its start with Sherman Poppen's Snurfers.

Resembling a small, plywood surfboard with a rope leash to help the rider balance, the Snurfer tended to hurtle down slopes in any direction it chose, and the rider had little control over the Snurfer's speed. Riding one was an experience not soon forgotten, and it paved the way for today's snowboards.

At about the same time that Poppen was designing the Snurfer, Tom Sims, a New Jersey teenager, had an idea. Frustrated because winter's icy streets prevented him from using his skateboard, he modified the basic skateboard design in his junior high school wood shop class to create a skateboard for ice.

His first designs weren't successful, but Sims kept experimenting. Finally, in 1969, he hit upon the right combination of shape, materials, and bindings. The sport of snowboarding was born, and Sims, who was living in California by then, began snowboard production. Today, Sims Snowboards are regularly seen at snowboard events and on ski slopes.

Poppen and Sims weren't alone in their quest to conquer the winter world of sports. A Vermont Snurfer named Jake Burton Carpenter began experimenting with the basic design of the Snurfer. Carpenter attached rubber straps to it and achieved better directional control. This led him to start a company to produce snowboards. Today, Burton Snowboards are very common on snowy mountain slopes.

It is from these humble beginnings that snowboarding springs. But the journey from Snurfer to legitimate sport hasn't been smooth.

Plagued in the early years by the Snurfer's reputation for unpredictability, snowboarding was outlawed at most ski resorts. Because a snowboard wasn't seen as a "directional device" like a pair of skis, insurance companies refused to write liability policies for resorts that allowed snowboarding. Resort operators didn't want to be held

While Snurfers were known for their unpredictability, today's snowboards allow for precision turns.

liable if a mishap occurred, so they had little choice but to deny snowboarders access to their slopes.

Snowboarding was also plagued by the reputation of those who were the first to enthusiastically take up the new sport—young surfers and skateboarders. Whether deserved or not, surfers and skateboarders were perceived as a rebellious group sure to flout the rules under which ski resorts must operate. Discrimination against them created friction and, for a time, the future of the sport was in jeopardy.

To promote American acceptance of the sport, Jake Burton Carpenter sponsored touring demonstration teams and local instruction programs. A certification program was begun that encouraged safety, proper technique, and slope etiquette, and snowboarding slowly gained respectability. As a result, snowboarders now can practice their sport at almost any ski resort in the United States and Canada as well as worldwide.

No longer is snowboarding solely a sport for surfers and skateboarders. With respectability came acceptance and broad-based appeal. An international series of competitive events called the World Cup and other regional contests have lured sponsors and advertisers to take the sport as seriously

Competitive snowboarding has lured many for whom traditional sports are unappealing.

as they do major league baseball or football. Today's snowboarders may be white-collar or no-collar; they may be single or an entire family. The sport's appeal crosses age lines and gender lines. Even die-hard skiers are racking their skis and taking up winter's one-time "outlaw" sport. It is not surprising, then, that snowboarding is the world's fastest-growing alpine sport.

Successful Simplicity

One reason for snowboarding's success is its pared-down simplicity. Unlike skiing, there is no need for special boots or poles. The basic piece of equipment is your snowboard. A snowboard and an experienced rider can descend a slope with a graceful, flowing motion that catches the eyes of onlookers.

Today's snowboards have come a long way from the Snurfer designed by Sherman Poppen. No longer made of plywood and rope, snowboards are designed to enhance safety and performance. They are constructed of laminated wood or fiberglass over foam cores and have steel edges to assist turning, or carving. They are faster, safer, and easier to handle than their forerunners.

The steel edges on a snowboard assist in turning, or carving.

Each designed for a different type of snowboarding, today's models typically fall into one of four categories: freestyle, freeride, freecarve, and racing. How do you choose which one is best for the type of riding you plan to do?

- Freestyle snowboards are built shorter, wider, and with more flexibility than other boards for the tricks and aerial stunts that riders are likely to perform in halfpipes—U-shaped trenches with walls of snow built up on either side—and snowboard parks. There are two categories of freestyle snowboards: halfpipe and slopestyle. A halfpipe board is built to flex with the curves of the pipe. Slopestyle boards are even more flexible to make it easier to perform skateboard-style stunts on the open slopes.

- Freeride snowboards are for general use. They combine characteristics of all the others and are a good choice if you plan to freestyle only part of the time. Some freeride boards are built extra long for the deep snow a rider will encounter when riding off-piste, or off the groomed slopes of resort areas.

- Freecarve boards are similar to racing boards, but they have more flex for riding under variable snow conditions.

- Racing boards, as the name implies, are for competition. They are narrow and designed for high-speed carving by putting more of the edge into contact with the snow's surface. (The amount of edge that comes into contact with the snow is called the effective edge, a term your sales person will probably use.) Racing boards are built stiff, with little flex, to maximize speed potential.

Modern technology has its price. While Snurfers sold for around $15 each, snowboards range from about $300 on up. Racing boards are the most expensive; you can expect to spend between $450 and $800 (or more!) for top-flight equipment geared to competition.

The only other necessary pieces of equipment are the binding and leash. The binding holds, or "binds," your foot to the snowboard. There are three binding types available: plate, high-back, and clicker. The type of binding you choose will be determined by the kind of boot you plan to wear and the snowboard activity you plan to pursue. The leash, usually a nylon strap, generally attaches to the front binding on one end and to your front leg (for most people this is the left leg) on the other. This leash prevents your snowboard from running away should your boots release from their bindings, and most ski resorts require them. When you are carrying your snowboard, loop the leash around your wrist.

A plate binding is a metal or hard plastic plate with a toe and heel fastener, or bail. It is designed to be used with hard-shell boots that have extended toes and heels. Plate bindings are the system of choice among racers because hard-shell boots offer them necessary ankle support.

Freestylers and others, on the other hand, usually choose high-back bindings. Made of rigid plastic, high-

Hard-shell boots are used with plate bindings. Note the extended toe and heel in the hard-shell boot. Soft boots are used with high-back bindings.

back bindings are designed to be used with soft boots, those usually having rubber bottoms and leather uppers. They fit over the boots and are secured with two or three buckle clips. Some freestylers "adjust" the fit by wrapping duct-tape around the tops of their boots. This provides them with more support than high-back bindings alone, but not enough to restrict movement.

The most recent development in binding systems is the clicker, a metal binding system that is rapidly gaining popularity. Designed to be worn with cleated boots, clicker bindings allow easier entry and better use of slope time. A snowboarder simply steps toe-first into the binding and then by clicking the heel down, the snowboard is locked in place and ready to go. The binding is released by a trigger at the side. Virtually every binding manufacturer will offer its own version of the clicker system beginning in the 1998 ski season.

Each binding system has its advantages and disadvantages. Before making a decision as to which type suits your needs, decide whether you'll be racing or freestyling. Consider, too, the cost. Plate and clicker bindings are typically more expensive than high-back bindings. Specialized boots for plate and clicker bindings are also an added expense. High-back bindings, while less expensive, tend to be fading in popularity among hard-core snowboarders. It is still, however, the most widely used binding and may be a good bet for a beginner.

In the end, you are the only person who can decide which snowboard and binding system is best. Ask other snowboarders what their preferences are. It is also a good idea to ride a variety of snowboards and to experiment with each binding system yourself. Then, make your own comparisons before making a purchase.

Techno-Talk Techno-Talk Techno-Talk

In the beginning you'll probably rent your equipment and have little interest in design innovations that help a snowboard to perform. When you are ready to purchase your own equipment, however, the terms listed below will help you match a snowboard to your style of riding.

Effective Edge--As mentioned elsewhere, the effective edge is simply the amount of a snowboard's edge that comes in contact with the snow's surface. A board with a longer effective edge grips the snow better.

Tip and Tail Kicks--An edge-view glimpse at a snowboard will reveal that its tip and tail curve, or kick, upward. This helps a board "float" over the snow instead of digging into it. Because racing boards are designed for downhill speed, most of the tail kick is eliminated. Freestylers, however, are as likely to ride forward as they are backward (called fakie) and so the tail kick on a freestyle board is often as pronounced as its tip kick.

Swing Weight--This term refers to how much force it takes to rotate a board in an aerial maneuver. Generally speaking, it takes more force to rotate a longer board because there's more of it extending beyond your feet. Because freestylers often perform airborne stunts, freestyle boards tend to be shorter than others.

Sidecut--Snowboards generally have an hourglass shape. That is, they are narrower at the middle than they are at the tip and tail. This arc shape is called sidecut. As a basic rule the deeper the sidecut, the sharper and tighter you can turn. A shallower sidecut, however, may hold the edge better.

There are many other technical terms—core construction, flex, camber, and symmetry, to name a few—but those defined here are of the most interest to beginning snowboarders who are making a purchase decision. If you get serious about snowboarding, especially competitive snowboarding, then you can broaden your knowledge of the other terms by checking some of the references listed at the back of this book.

Dressing for Success

Even with the best snowboard and perfect bindings and boots, a snowboarding experience can be a disaster if you aren't dressed for the environment. While clothing projects image, it also protects against the cold—something snowy mountain slopes seem to have in endless supply. If you are unprepared and underdressed, scenic slopes can be harsh, brutal, and unforgiving.

Because temperatures often dip to zero degrees Fahrenheit (-18°C) and colder at higher elevations, snowboarders often wear insulated ski clothing. When warm weather ski conditions prevail, usually in the spring, you will find snowboarders wearing anything from ragged blue jeans and decorative scarves to "surfer" shorts and tie-dyed T-shirts.

A beginning snowboarder should be insulated and padded for an enjoyable and safe experience.

Comfort is the key factor. When you race, the temperature will always seem colder as you zip down a course at 70 miles per hour (113 km/hr) or more. When you participate in freestyle, on the other hand, be concerned with clothing that won't restrict movement. It's the only way you'll be able to execute incredible stunts.

Mountain temperatures and conditions are often unpredictable. What may begin as a beautiful, sunny morning may turn into a blizzard before you make your last run. It's better to store clothing in a locker if you get too warm than to freeze for lack of good judgment or for the sake of style. Be prepared for the worst, and modify as conditions permit.

Pants

In the very beginning, you'll spend a lot of time on your rear, knees, and hands. Choose pants that are water and wind resistant. Jeans, although popular, aren't a wise choice for a beginning snowboarder because they tend to absorb moisture. Nothing is more chilling than zooming down a mountain in wet pants! Opt instead for ski pants or for snowboarding pants, which have reinforced seats and knees. Under these, wear a thin, close-fitting layer of long underwear. Long underwear made of high-tech fabrics such as polypropylene will insulate your body better than long underwear made of cotton. It will also wick moisture away from your skin, lessening the chance of chill.

Jackets

When you participate in any winter activity, you should wear multiple layers of clothing. This will keep you warmer and also allow you to adjust for temperature changes. Jackets should be water resistant and roomy enough to allow for this layered approach. Just be sure that the cuffs, waist, and neck don't gap. Under your jacket, wear a wool or fleece pullover sweater or possibly a vest.

Gloves

Either snowboarding gloves or ski gloves will keep your hands warm. The only difference is that snowboarding gloves usually have longer cuffs that fit snugly over your jacket sleeve to keep out the snow. Snowboarding gloves designed for racing have extra padding across the back to deflect slalom gates painlessly. Good gloves are expensive, but worth the investment. Avoid leather and knitted gloves. Neither type provides adequate protection against the cold. Synthetic products, such as Gore-Tex, are a better choice. Tip: Mittens will keep your fingers warmer than gloves. Also, glove liners made of silk or capilene will help keep your hands toasty.

Gloved hands sometimes help stabilize a turn.

Goggles

A good pair of goggles or tinted glasses will protect your eyes from wind, precipitation, glare, and ultraviolet (UV) radiation. The best goggles are designed to improve contrast in poor visibility. They come single and double-lensed. The double-lensed variety reduces the chances of fogging, though even the best may fog under some conditions.

Hats

Wearing a hat will help your entire body stay warmer. A variety of hat styles made of different materials exists. Whether knitted or fitted, wool or acrylic, the hat you choose should be comfortable. If keeping your ears warm is a problem, select a hat with earflaps. Some hats have ties under the chin to keep them from blowing off. If your hat doesn't have chin ties, invest in a hat catcher, a short leash that clips to the hat on one end and to the collar of your jacket on the other end.

Sunscreen

Any exposed skin needs to be protected with sunscreen. At higher altitudes, the sun's UV rays are more intense. This, coupled with the reflection from the snow, can cause severe burn and extreme discomfort—even on cloudy days. Wear a sunscreen of at least factor fifteen and reapply it periodically during the day. Protect your lips with lip balm. Keep in mind that early and late in the season, the sun is especially strong.

The Rules of the Road

Snowboarding's road to acceptance has been long and difficult. Part of the reason that it was successful in its efforts to gain acceptance, and even encouragement, is that snowboarders began to monitor themselves and their behavior. Seeking to win over skiers and resort operators, they implemented a snowboarding code that stressed safety and consideration. While there is still the odd snowboarder who careens carelessly down ski slopes, today's breed of snowboarder shuns such reckless behavior. They understand that observance of a few rules guarantees that everyone—snowboarders and skiers alike—will have an enjoyable, safe experience on the slopes.

One of the ways a snowboarder controls the speed of descent is by leaning forward or backward.

Most of the snowboarding code is based on common courtesy, treating others the way you hope to be treated in return. If you act according to the code, you will have no problem challenging the mountain time and time again. But if you choose to ignore it, you may be asked to leave the mountain, and you may jeopardize today's peaceful coexistence between skiers and snowboarders.

Courtesy and common sense usually are closely related. Skipping ahead in a lift line, for example, might seem like a quick way to get back to the top of the mountain for another run. But everyone else in line wants to get to the top of the mountain, too. If you don't like it when people cut in front of you, then don't do it to others.

Sometimes people fall when getting off a lift. In fact, it probably happens to everyone sooner or later. But some people just lie where they fall, laughing at their awkwardness. It is no laughing matter if you happen to be getting off the lift behind them. Take a minute to think about the others using the area. Most hazards and awkward situations can be avoided by employing a little thought and responsible action.

The code exists so that everyone—both snowboarders and skiers—will have a safe and enjoyable experience on the mountain. Although there are many variations of it, the basic messages are the same.

- Always wear a snowboard leash.

- Don't make unpredictable maneuvers without glancing behind you to make certain you are not being overtaken by another snowboarder or a skier.

- A person who is downhill always has the right of way. If you plan to pass, assume that you have not been seen and alert him or her by announcing, "On your left," or "On your right."

- Never cross in front of another person too closely.

- Do not stop in a bottleneck or narrow stretch. Move to the side so that anyone approaching will have a clear path. If you fall, move to the side as quickly as you can.

- Do not stop just below the crest of a hill where you cannot be seen by anyone approaching.

- Never pass through a snowboard or ski class.

- Observe ski patrol signs.

- Don't show off.

- Allow skiers the right of way.

- If someone in your party sustains an injury, don't move the injured person. If the injured person is not plainly visible, ask someone to stand a distance uphill to serve as a warning to anyone approaching. Then use the emergency phones common to most resorts to contact the ski patrol. Be certain you can identify the name of the run the injured person is on and the approximate location.

This snowboarder's leash will prevent a runaway board.

Freestylers take their turn one by one in the halfpipe.

If you are a freestyler, know that halfpipes also require courtesy. Mutual consideration is the key factor:

- Take your run in turn.

- Begin your run by announcing, "Dropping." (You are "dropping" into the halfpipe.)

- One snowboarder at a time is best. Congestion in a halfpipe might interfere with someone's freestyle performance. It can also be dangerous. Imagine what might happen if two or more snowboarders collided at speeds of 40 miles per hour (64 km/hr) or greater.

- When you finish your run, exit the halfpipe; don't linger at the bottom.

- If you are observing, stay well back from the rim of the halfpipe. Freestylers can and do execute stunts along the rim.

Snowboarding is challenging. It's exciting. By being a responsible snowboarder who adheres to the code, you make the mountain a safer place for everybody using it.

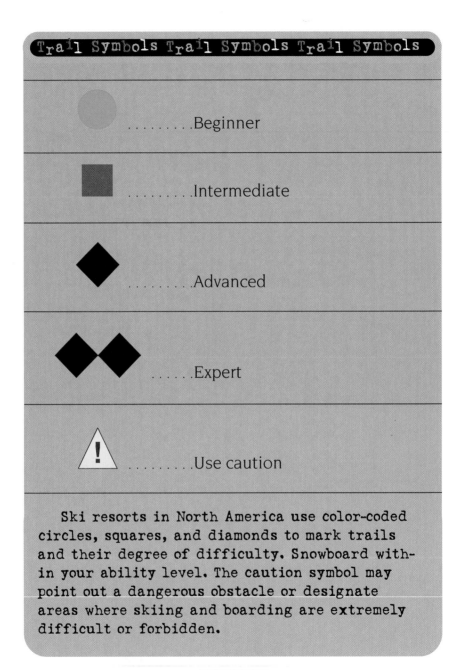

.........Beginner

.........Intermediate

.........Advanced

......Expert

.........Use caution

Ski resorts in North America use color-coded circles, squares, and diamonds to mark trails and their degree of difficulty. Snowboard within your ability level. The caution symbol may point out a dangerous obstacle or designate areas where skiing and boarding are extremely difficult or forbidden.

Avoiding Injury

No sport is guaranteed to be injury-free. Snow-boarding is no exception. The most common snow-boarding accidents are injuries to the wrists, thumbs, and upper body. And the best way to avoid such an injury is to learn how to fall. Although this may sound strange because most people have ample experience with falling, there actually is a correct and an incorrect way to fall.

When most beginning snowboarders fall, they tend to catch themselves by planting their hands palm down in the snow. This is the incorrect way to fall, as it puts pressure on the wrist or thumb and may cause a fracture or break. The correct and safer method of falling is to try to break your fall with the fleshy part of your forearms if falling forward or on your rear if falling backward.

While nobody plans to fall, the fact is that no one mounts a snowboard for the first time without taking a few spills. And chances are, you'll take more than a few. But stick with it. Get up. Dust off the snow. Then try again to get the technique right.

Begin by becoming certified. Some ski resorts refuse snowboarders access to the lifts unless they have proof of certification, usually a small identification card. In a certification class, you will learn the proper techniques of on-loading and off-loading a ski lift. You'll also learn how to stop—a vital skill on a congested ski slope. Finally, and perhaps most importantly, your instructor will pay attention to how well you fall and correct your technique if necessary.

You will want to get a feel for the snowboard before attending a certification class. Begin by practicing on the "bunny slopes," those areas that have a shallow incline and can be reached on foot. Be certain that your practice area is free of any obstacles or exposed rocks that might be hazardous. Avoid congested areas. The last thing you want to do is run over somebody or have somebody run over you. Besides, the smaller your audience, the more comfortable you'll be—especially if you fall. And you will.

Time and practice are essential to learning snow-boarding, and not everyone has equal ability. Learn at your own rate. Some may learn more quickly; others, more slowly. The rate at which you learn is not as important as how well you learn. Listen to yourself. You'll know when you're ready for greater challenges.

It's difficult to imagine anyone venturing into the snow without winter clothing. As a beginner, you'll spend as much or more time *in* the snow as *on* it. Winter clothing helps to keep you warm and dry. It also helps to provide additional padding to absorb the jolts you'll most likely experience from falling.

Remember that snowboarding is a demanding, aggressive sport. Don't practice it if you are tired. Be rested. If you have to ask yourself if you have the energy to make it down the mountain one more time, you are probably too tired to attempt another run. Take a break and come back to it fresh. Accidents and fatigue go hand in hand, so don't tempt fate by pushing yourself too hard.

Snowboarding in the back country, or off-piste, is gaining in popularity. It's a unique sensation to carve through fresh-fallen snow, but there is an ever-present danger when you venture from a resort's groomed runs: avalanche. It is best that beginners and intermediates stick to the groomed slopes. When you do venture off-piste, be sure to go with a friend or two and check with the ski patrol to determine which areas are safe and legal.

Snowboarding can be fun and safe. Surprisingly, there are *fewer* accidents, by percentage, on snowboards than

Snowboarding off-piste, or off the groomed slopes, offers great thrills . . .

on skis. It is believed that this is because snowboarding involves only one piece of equipment, the snowboard. When snowboarders fall, they do so in one neat pile, without the tangle of arms, legs, skis, and poles that downed skiers often experience.

Responsible behavior. Practice. Control. It all adds up to safe snowboarding.

but it also carries its own hazards.

Experienced snowboarders can handle a variety of
trails and conditions, such as steep slopes and
deep snow.

Getting Started

Whatever the endeavor, ability is usually dependent on time and practice. Snowboarding is no different. The more time you spend practicing, the better you'll become. The snowboarders you see in television commercials and movies didn't learn their skills overnight. They practiced until they got it right—and continue to hone their skills by practicing even more. Take heart. With a little pluck and a lot of practice, you'll be carving with the best of them.

So, how does a promising snowboarder get started? One of the first things you'll determine is whether you are regular-footed or goofy-footed, terms borrowed from surfing. If you're regular-footed, you'll snowboard with your left foot forward. If you're goofy, you'll naturally favor your right foot in the forward position. This is your stance.

This snowboarder is goofy-footed.

How do you determine if you're regular or goofy? If you've ever ridden a skateboard or surfboard, then you already know which stance is natural for you. If not, then use the same stance you would to bat a baseball. Perhaps you've never played baseball or softball. Then pretend that you're sliding across a slippery floor. Which foot do you lead with? This is probably the foot you'll want to place at the front of the snowboard.

The next thing to figure out is your stance width and angle. The stance width is how far apart you position your feet. There is nothing carved in stone about this. Stand in a natural, comfortable way. For most people, stance width falls between 16 and 24 inches (40 and 60 cm) apart. The stance angle is the angle of your feet across the board, since you ride a snowboard in a sideways fashion. Again, choose an angle that is comfortable. Both width and angle are important for determining binding placement and adjustment. If you find that you experience toe or heel drag—your toes or heels extend beyond the edge of the board into the snow—it will interfere with your performance. There are several remedies:

1. Buy or rent a wider board that will accommodate your feet.
2. Adjust your stance angle until your toes or heels do not extend beyond the board's edge.
3. Insert lift plates between the binding and the deck to raise your toes or heels.

Basic Skills

So, now you're ready to conquer the slopes—the "bunny" slopes. Snowboarding is really about balancing on your front foot while steering with your rear foot. And suc-

A toeside turn

cessful balancing is built upon three basic skills: edging, pivoting, and pressure control.

Edging is tilting the board to the frontside (toe) or backside (heel) edge. Tilting a board on either edge while slipping along the snow makes the board turn. The more exaggerated your tilt, the sharper your turn.

Pivoting the board, using your front foot as the pivot point, is the way low-speed turns are executed. The rear foot "kicks" the board left or right to change the direction of the board.

Pressure control is the skill of increasing and decreasing weight along the board. This is accomplished either by raising or lowering your torso for pivoting or leaning slightly toeside or heelside for edging.

Before putting these theories into practice, however, there are some other skills you should know that will help you get around when there is minimal slope. The snowboard shuffle is similar to pushing a scooter. With your front foot in its binding and with your weight over it, push with your free back foot. Your snowboard will slide forward. Repeat the process. When you're ready to test your balance, you can try skating. Skating is similar to the snowboard shuffle, but instead of push-slide-push-slide you'll push-and-glide. In other words, as you push with your free back foot and the snowboard begins to move forward under its own momentum, rest your rear foot on the stomp pad, the rubber or plastic mat between the two bindings, and glide for a distance.

Walking uphill is another trick to master. To walk uphill, you'll need to determine where the fall line is. This is the imaginary line that follows the steepest part of any slope, the path a ball would tend to take if you rolled it downhill. To walk uphill, position your snowboard perpendicular to the fall line and dig its toe edge into the snow. Step uphill with your free foot. Then drag the snowboard uphill behind you. (Imagine a prisoner dragging a ball on a chain.) Replant the toe edge of the snowboard

Sometimes the trip uphill takes a little effort, but it's worth it.

into the snow, and take another step uphill. Step-drag, step-drag!

In lieu of walking uphill in the step-drag manner, you can also hop. This froglike maneuver is done with both feet strapped into the bindings. Position the snowboard perpendicular to the fall line and dig in the toe edge. Pull your knees up to your chest, and spring forward. Hop! Hop! Hop!

Once you're at the top, gravity can take over and you

can enjoy the ride down. That is, after all, why you went to all that effort to gain some elevation!

Riding Downhill

Your first rides downhill should be straight glides just to help you become acquainted with the feel of skimming over snow. Stand in the "ready position"—knees slightly bent, arms outstretched about waist high, looking and pointing in the direction you wish to travel. Gravity will start your downhill movement. As you descend, rest your free rear foot on the stomp pad and try to maintain your balance. Your weight should be over your front foot since the weighted end of your snowboard will descend the slope first. If too much weight is over your rear foot, you may find yourself doing a fakie—descending the slope backward!

If you fall, try to break your fall with your forearms or rear. Also, try to keep your loose foot on the snowboard. It will be good practice for when both feet are strapped into your bindings.

Doing a straight glide on a shallow incline is also a good time to practice stopping. Stopping, as you might guess, is a basic and highly important skill to know. Anybody will tell you that one of the easiest ways to stop is to sit. Graphically called the "butt drop," it's usually effective, if not graceful. But depending on the quality of the snow you're landing on, it can be rough on your body.

The alternative is the side-slip, or snowplow. To side-slip, turn your snowboard perpendicular to the fall line and dig in the uphill edge. The side-slip can be done backward (toes pointing uphill) or forward. The key to remember is that stopping is dependent on digging in the uphill edge, whether that is toeside or heelside.

Turning

Straight glides are good practice, but eventually you'll want to turn left or right, either to avoid something ahead of you or to make the ride more interesting. Snow-boarders use three types of turns: skidded turns, carved turns, and jump turns.

Skidded turns use the feet to control direction. Think of your front foot as the gas pedal and the rear foot as the brake. To accelerate, position your weight over the front foot. To turn, look in the direction you wish to turn, point, and press your rear foot downhill. Skidded turns lead to carved turns.

Carved turns are similar to skidded turns. The difference is in the tilting action of the foot, which puts the board on edge and causes the board to slice gracefully through the snow. To make a toeside turn, shift your weight over the balls of your feet. A heelside turn shifts the weight over the heels.

Jump turns are exactly what you imagine. You turn,

Practice and experience pay off with skill.

or "kick," the board while you're airborne, the rear foot dictating the direction of the turn.

The secret to executing smooth, professional turns is practice. Don't expect to master them your first day on the slopes. But keep at it. Don't give up. Eventually, you'll be linking turns and traversing the slope. And that's what snowboarding is all about.

Although there are other means of getting to mountain tops—rope tows, t-bars, poma lifts, and others—chairlifts provide a restful ride and are one of the most common means of accessing a resort's runs. Even so, they may be intimidating to the novice snowboarder. Exactly how do you negotiate a moving chair when there's a snowboard strapped to one of your feet?

If you are not experienced with chairlifts, be sure to tell the lift attendants that it's your first time. They will slow the lift for you to allow you plenty of time to get seated.

Just as soon as the party ahead of you has been seated and swept away, be prepared to move rapidly into the loading zone. Don't panic! Just use the snowboard shuffle to get into the loading zone and position yourself on the wait marker. Then look over your shoulder—to the left if you're sitting on the left side of a two-person chair, to the right if you're sitting on the right side. (Some chairs carry more than two people. If you happen to be seated in the middle, look over whichever shoulder is most comfortable.) As the chair approaches, slow its motion with your hand as you sit down. That was easy, wasn't it?

On your way up the mountain, you'll have a snowboard dangling from one foot. It will be more comfortable for you if you allow it to rest on your free foot. This will help prevent your leg and foot from cramping or falling asleep.

To off-load, watch for signs that announce the approach of the end of the lift. Look for the exit path well in advance of actually off-loading so you can calculate the maneuvers you'll have to make. Then as your snowboard comes in contact with the snow, push yourself to a standing position with your hands and glide down the ramp, your weight over your front foot and your free foot resting on the stomp pad.

Stop off to the side, well out of the path of those who will be unloading behind you. Strap your free foot into its binding. Adjust your gloves and goggles. And get set for your downhill adventure.

With their back feet resting on the stomp pad, these snowboarders glide away from the chairlift.

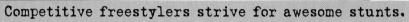
Competitive freestylers strive for awesome stunts.

Competition

Snowboarding, like many other hobbies, has a fiercely competitive side. Some young snowboarders begin competing shortly after their first successful downhill run. Competition lets snowboarders combine pressure with speed, balance, and control. Often, the competition is informal, with friends getting together to race or compare stunts. At other times, the events are officially sanctioned by the Professional Snowboarders Association of North America, the United States Amateur Snowboarding Association, or some other sponsoring organization. They offer competitors prizes, trophies, and money.

The world of freestyle snowboarding is about performing stunts on the snow or in the air. It's a mix of snowboarder, acrobat, and choreographer. You may have already begun your freestyle career by performing stunts unintentionally when you were first learning to snowboard! Competitive freestylers, however, perform for judges who mark their stunts for degree of difficulty and

A freestyler "catches air."

the skill with which they were performed. Style counts, so freestylers put a lot of personality and attitude into their routines. Depending on which organization is sanctioning the competition, there will be three to five judges who will be looking at specific judging criteria—everything from how high the freestyler launches (amplitude) to how smoothly he or she lands (landings). To succeed in the top ranks of freestyle competition, you must be a first-rate athlete in top shape.

Alpine snowboard racing takes its cue from skiing. It is less about style and more about speed—a downhill

A racer zips past a gate in the slalom.

race against the clock and/or an opponent. Events include the super G, giant slalom (GS), parallel GS, slalom, and the parallel slalom. Although the International Snowboard Federation has set the course standards for the different racing events, other amateur and professional snowboarding organizations frequently modify those standards. Before entering a race it is a good idea to review the sponsoring organization's rules so you won't be taken by surprise.

Snowboarding competition doesn't end there. One alpine-type event that has become popular in recent years is Boardercross®. It's motocross without the dirt and cycles, and tends to put alpine racers on an equal footing with freestylers since a typical course will include everything from aerial jumps to slalom gates.

Figure-eight competitions are about symmetry. Using fresh, untracked snow, figure eights begin when two snowboarders are air lifted to the top of a slope. Their goal is to make synchronized figure eights all the way back to the valley floor. Judging is based on the symmetry of the figure eights left in the snow and on the synchronism of the two snowboarders.

Obstacle courses are new to snowboarding competition. These are timed events that have individual racers competing one at a time and completing a course over jumps and through quarterpipes (halfpipes with only one

No, it's not a skateboard! A snowboarder "grinding" on a rail.

wall). The goal is to survive the obstacles and get to the bottom of the course faster than anybody else.

In 1992, something new entered the world of snowboard competition: the World Extreme Championships in Valdez, Alaska. The premise behind an extreme competition is to fly a pack of fearless riders to the most rugged terrain imaginable. They pick a course that they think will impress judges and then, one at a time, make their

descent. Judges look at everything from the aggressiveness with which the chosen course is tackled to the amount of time a rider remains airborne. To most of us, extreme competitions look crazy, but it gives those who participate in them a chance to push the limits.

Whatever the event, freestyle or racing, competition will give you a chance to test your skills against the skills of others. It will also give you a chance to witness firsthand some of the very best that snowboarding has to offer. Just don't lose sight of what snowboarding has been about ever since the days of the Snurfer—fun!

Several organizations sponsor competitive snowboarding events. To compete for prizes and money, you often have to belong to the sponsoring organization. Several are listed below.

Canadian Snowboard Federation
2440, Place Prevel Apt. 8
Sainte-Foy, Quebec G1V 2X3
Canada

International Snowboard Federation
PO Box 477
Vail, CO 81658

Professional Snowboarders Association of North
  America
PO Box 477
Vail, CO 81658

United States Amateur Snowboarding Association
PO Box 4400
Frisco, CO 80443

United States Ski Association—Snowboarding
PO Box 100
Park City, UT 84060

For more information about the sport of snowboarding, techniques for specific freestyle stunts, and alpine racing rules, try these other sources. Some will be available at your school, public library, or snowboard supply shop. Others will take a little more effort to find.

Magazines

Eastern Edge Snowboarding Magazine
PO Box 79
Alpine, NJ 07620

Snowboarder
PO Box 1028
Dana Point, CA 92629

Snowboard U.K.
Air Publications, Unit 1a Franchise Street
Kidderminster, Worcestershire DY10 6RE
England

Transworld Snowboarding Magazine
353 Airport Road
Oceanside, CA 92054

Books

Bennett, Jeff, and Scott Downey. *The Complete Snowboarder*. Camden, Maine: Ragged Mountain Press, 1994.

Reichenfeld, Rob, and Anna Bruechert. *Snowboarding*. Champaign, Ill.: Human Kinetics Publishers, Inc., 1995.

Because of the changeable nature of the Internet, sites appear and disappear very quickly. These resources offered useful information on snowboarding at the time of publication. Internet addresses must be entered with capital and lowercase letters exactly as they appear.

Yahoo!
http://www.yahoo.com/
The *Yahoo!* directory on the World Wide Web is an excellent place to find Internet sites on any topic.

GoSki!
http://www.goski.com/
This online guide to snow sports includes information on (and links to) resorts, gear, and travel. *GoSki!* also features the latest news on snow sports including snow reports at mountains worldwide.

SkiCentral—Search & Index Site for Skiers & Snowboarders
http://www.skicentral.com
SkiCentral, is a comprehensive snowboarding and skiing resource on the Internet, indexing 3,300 sites. The site includes a powerful and easy-to-use search engine to

help you find sites on many different aspects of snow-boarding.

SkiNet
http://www.skinet.com
SkiNet is the online presence of *Ski* and *Skiing* magazines. The site offers much information on snowboarding including tips on technique, news, equipment reviews, resort and travel information, and forums for discussing snowboarding issues with other snowboarders.

Index Index Index Index Index Index Index

LARRY DANE BRIMNER has written many First Books for Franklin Watts, including *Surfing, Rock Climbing, Mountain Biking, Karate,* and *Rolling . . . In-line.* He is also the author of several Watts books for older readers, including *Letters to Our Children,* and *Voices from the Camps: Internment of Japanese Americans During World War* II. When he isn't writing, Mr. Brimner visits elementary schools throughout the country to discuss the writing process with young authors and readers.